Country File
The Caribbean

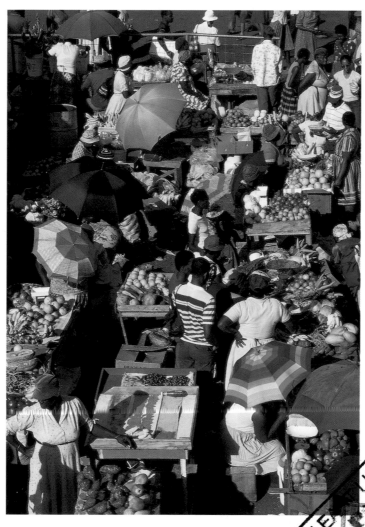

Ian Graham

W
FRANKLIN WATTS
LONDON•SYDNEY

Revised and updated 2005

Franklin Watts
96 Leonard Street, London
EC2A 4XD

Franklin Watts Australia
Level 17/207 Kent Street
Sydney NSW 2000

COUNTRY FILE: THE CARIBBEAN produced for Franklin Watts by Bender Richardson White, PO Box 266, Uxbridge, UK.
Project Editor: Lionel Bender
Text Editor: Peter Harrison
Designer: Ben White
Picture Researcher: Cathy Stastny
Media Conversion and Make-up: Mike Pilley, Radius
Production: Kim Richardson

Graphics: Mike Pilley, Radius
Maps: Stefan Chabluk

For Franklin Watts:
Series Editor: Adrian Cole
Art Director: Jonathan Hair

A CIP catalogue record for this book is available from the British Library.

ISBN 0 7496 6417 7

Dewey classification 917.29

Printed in China

Picture Credits

Note to parents and teachers

Every effort has been made by the Publishers to ensure that the websites in this book are suitable for children, that they are of the highest educational value, and that they contain no inappropriate or offensive material. However, because of the nature of the Internet, it is impossible to guarantee that the contents of these sites will not be altered. We strongly advise that Internet access is supervised by a responsible adult.

The Author

Ian Graham is a full-time writer and editor of non-fiction books. He has written more than 100 books for children.

Contents

Welcome to the Caribbean

The Caribbean, or West Indies, is known to most people for its blue skies, white beaches, tropical palms and crystal-clear sea. It is an area of many islands with different cultures and traditions.

The region includes the Caribbean Sea and the island chain that separates it from the Atlantic Ocean. The chain stretches 3,200 kilometres, from North to South America.

Island chains

The islands fall into three main archipelagos (groups): the Greater Antilles, Lesser Antilles and Bahamas. Trinidad & Tobago and Barbados lie to the south and east of the Lesser Antilles but are not considered to be part of them.

The Greater Antilles consists of the four largest Caribbean islands: Cuba, Hispaniola (shared by Haiti and the Dominican Republic), Jamaica and Puerto Rico.

This book concentrates on the islands that were former British colonies: Jamaica, Barbados, the Bahamas, Trinidad & Tobago and most of the smaller islands of the Lesser Antilles.

DATABASE

The Lesser Antilles are split into two groups, the Windward Islands and Leeward Islands.

Guadeloupe and Martinique are sometimes known as the 'French Antilles'. They are Overseas Regions of France.

Guyana, formerly a British colony, is on the mainland of South America but is regarded as part of the Caribbean. With a land area of 215,000 square kilometres it is the largest country in the Caribbean.

The fishing port of Soufrière on St. Lucia, one of the Windward Islands. Surrounded by palms, Soufrière is the island's main centre of coconut production. ▼

VIRGIN IS.
St. Kitts
and Nevis
Codrington ○ **Barbuda**
St. John's
Basseterre ○ ○ **Antigua**
Plymouth ○ **Montserrat**
Pointe-à-Pitre ○
○ **Guadeloupe**

Roseau ○ **Dóminica**

Fort-de-France ○ **Martinique**

Castries ○ **St. Lucia**

Bridgetown ○ **Barbados**
Kingstown ○
**St. Vincent and
the Grenadines**

St. George's ○ **Grenada**

Tobago

○ Port of Spain
Trinidad

*ATLANTIC
OCEAN*

LESSER ANTILLES

Mountains

Grassland and farming

○ Major city

Country boundary

0   500 Miles

0   750 Kilometres

0   100 Miles

0   100 Kilometres

80°W   75°W

USA

*GULF
OF
MEXICO*

25°N

**BAHAMA
ISLANDS**

Nassau ○

Andros I.

Tropic of Cancer

La Habana ○

CUBA

Isla de la
Juventud

G R E A T E R

CAYMAN IS.

Great
Inagua

**TURKS and
CAICOS ISLANDS**

70°W   65°W   60°W   20°N

ATLANTIC OCEAN

**DOMINICAN
REPUBLIC**
HAITI
Port-au-Prince ○
Santo
Domingo

San Juan
○
**PUERTO
RICO**

VIRGIN IS.
**St. Kitts
and Nevis**
Montserrat

LEEWARD ISLANDS
Barbuda
Antigua
Guadeloupe

JAMAICA
Kingston ○

A N T I L L E S

Dóminica   15°N

Martinique

St. Lucia

Barbados

**St. Vincent and
the Grenadines**

WINDWARD ISLANDS

CARIBBEAN SEA

L E S S E R

Grenada

Netherlands
Antilles

A N T I L L E S

Tobago   10°N

Trinidad

N
W   E
S

ONDURAS

ARAGUA

STA RICA

PANAMA   **COLOMBIA**   **VENEZUELA**   **GUYANA**
Georgetown ○

The Land

The steady, warm temperatures of the Caribbean islands can be accompanied by heavy rain. All the year round, daytime temperatures are around 25° to 30 °C at sea level, or slightly cooler in the mountains. Night-time temperatures rarely fall below 15 °C.

Moist air blowing in from the Atlantic Ocean makes some of the islands very humid, especially between June and November (the wet season). Some of the Leeward Islands receive as much as 8,890 millimetres of rain each year, while the islands closest to the South American coast may receive as little as 250 millimetres. Violent tropical storms and hurricanes can strike any time between July and October, although the southernmost islands are usually spared the devastating effects.

Volcanic islands

The Caribbean islands vary widely in size. The Bahamas have a total area of 13,940 square kilometres, for example, while Anguilla is only 91 square kilometres. The largest islands are the most mountainous.

Many of the islands have active or dormant volcanoes such as the twin peaks of the Pitons, a familiar landmark on St. Lucia in the Windward Islands. One of the most active volcanoes in the region is Mount Soufrière on St. Vincent, a former British colony at the southern end of the Windward Islands. Mount Soufrière erupted in 1812, 1902, 1971 and 1979, when most of the island had to be evacuated.

Animal Life

Lizards and snakes are found on all the Caribbean islands but only Trinidad has a variety of mammals, including monkeys and sloths. The most colourful creatures are the birds, especially parrots and hummingbirds. The sea teems with life, too. Coral reefs along the islands' eastern coasts are home to more than 1,000 species of fish.

Periodic rainfall maintains the lush vegetation on the island of St. Vincent. St. Vincent's plant life includes coconut palms, hibiscus and poinsettia. ▼

Weather

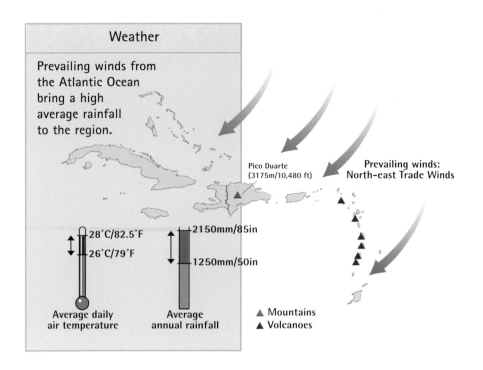

Prevailing winds from the Atlantic Ocean bring a high average rainfall to the region.

Pico Duarte (3175m/10,480 ft)

Prevailing winds: North-east Trade Winds

28°C/82.5°F
26°C/79°F

Average daily air temperature

+2150mm/85in
1250mm/50in

Average annual rainfall

▲ Mountains
▲ Volcanoes

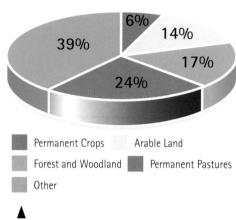

6%
14%
17%
24%
39%

Permanent Crops   Arable Land
Forest and Woodland   Permanent Pastures
Other

▲
▲ The main uses to which land is put in Jamaica.

Average monthly rainfall in Kingston, Jamaica. ▼

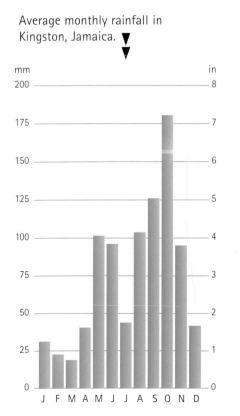

mm		in
200		8
175		7
150		6
125		5
100		4
75		3
50		2
25		1
0	J F M A M J J A S O N D	0

Average monthly temperatures in Kingston, Jamaica. ▼

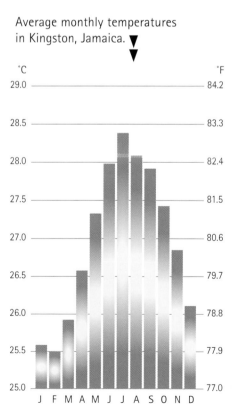

°C		°F
29.0		84.2
28.5		83.3
28.0		82.4
27.5		81.5
27.0		80.6
26.5		79.7
26.0		78.8
25.5		77.9
25.0	J F M A M J J A S O N D	77.0

Web Search ►►

► http://www.barbados.org/weather.htm
Barbadian weather and climate.

► http://www.go-jamaica.com/weather/maps.php
Current weather in Jamaica.

► http://www.caribwx.com/climate1.html
British Virgin Islands' climate.

► http://www.caribbeanvolcanoes.com
Information about the volcanoes of the Caribbean.

► http://www.worldclimate.com
World climate information.

The People

A s a result of the area's stormy history of invasion and slavery the Caribbean is populated by people from many different ethnic backgrounds. Few of the Caribbean's original inhabitants remain. The many different languages spoken reflect the wide range of places from which Caribbean people's ancestors came.

Most of the 38.8 million people who live in the Caribbean today are descended from those brought from West Africa in the 16th and 17th centuries to work as slaves on sugar plantations. The native Caribbean people were almost completely wiped out by European invaders.

Origins

The Caribbean is named after the Carib Indians. They lived in the Lesser Antilles when the first Spanish explorers arrived in the 15th century. The warlike Caribs had driven out the islands' original inhabitants, the Arawak Indians.

People from many different ethnic backgrounds mingle at a street market on Curaçao, in the Lesser Antilles. The first inhabitants of the Caribbean were Arawak Indians. ▼

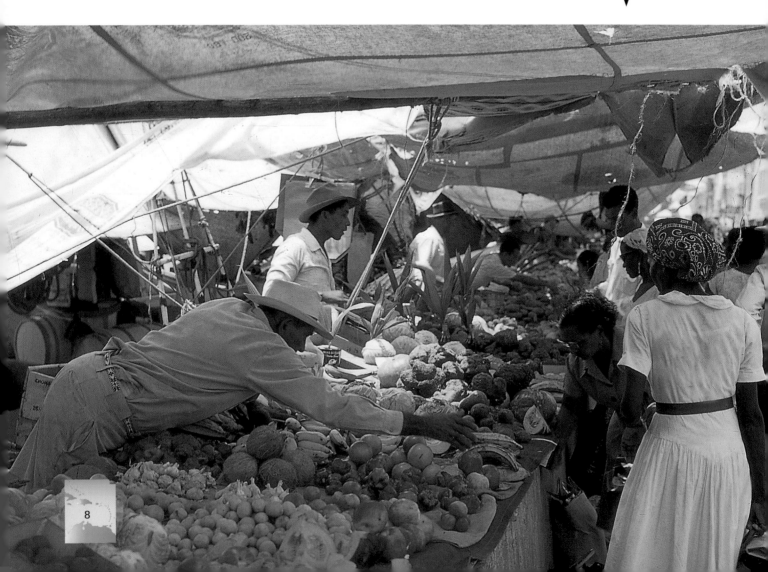

Many languages

A wide range of languages are spoken in the Caribbean today. Many people still speak the languages of the European countries that colonized the islands including Spanish, English, French and Dutch. Slaves developed their own versions of these languages, called *pidgin* and *creole*.

A second wave of settlers arrived in the 19th century and brought new languages such Hindi, Urdu and Chinese. Immigrants from India and their descendants became known as East Indians to distinguish them from the existing Caribbean people, or West Indians.

One language from six

Some of the Caribbean languages spoken today are combinations of as many as six other languages. *Papiemento* is spoken in Aruba and the Netherlands Antilles. It includes words taken from Spanish, Portuguese, English, Dutch and African languages, as well as from the local native language.

▲ Population figures for some of the islands in the Caribbean.

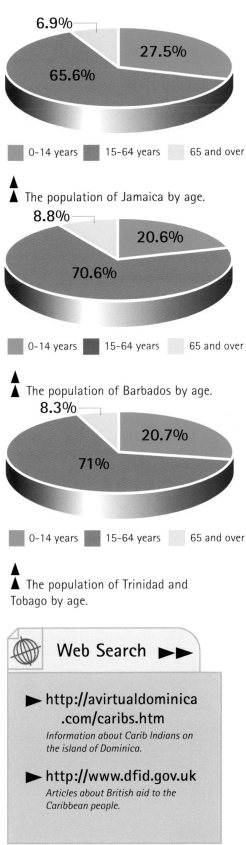

▲ The population of Jamaica by age.

▲ The population of Barbados by age.

▲ The population of Trinidad and Tobago by age.

Web Search ►►

► http://avirtualdominica
.com/caribs.htm
Information about Carib Indians on the island of Dominica.

► http://www.dfid.gov.uk
Articles about British aid to the Caribbean people.

Urban and Rural Life

Before the rapid growth in tourism and trade, most of the region's inhabitants worked in agriculture. Now, over half the population lives in urban areas. Fewer people live in rural villages and work the land.

Towns and cities throughout the Caribbean grew dramatically during the last century. More and more people left the countryside, hoping to find better jobs and more comfortable living conditions in urban areas. Despite this, Caribbean cities remain relatively small. Only a handful have populations of more than a million people.

A few of the largest cities have busy, multi-lane roads lined with high-rise office blocks, but most are less developed. The region's picturesque coastal towns are popular with tourists. Yachts line the modern marinas and cruise liners dock at the quays. Grand buildings and imposing monuments from the colonial era still stand in many places, giving the towns an historic flavour.

 Kingston, Jamaica

Almost half a million people live in the Jamaican capital, Kingston, and about 104,000 more in the surrounding suburbs.

Kingston was founded in 1692 and built to a neat grid system. Its name means 'king's town' and honours the British king, William III.

Jamaica became a British colony in 1655. At Port Royal, 17th-century cannons still point out to sea. They were there to defend the island against Dutch, Spanish or French attack.

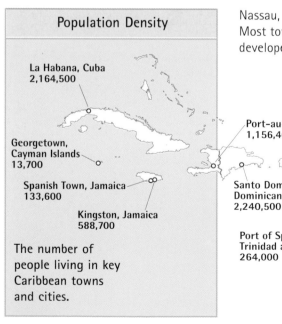

Population Density

La Habana, Cuba
2,164,500

Georgetown,
Cayman Islands
13,700

Spanish Town, Jamaica
133,600

Kingston, Jamaica
588,700

Port-au-Prince, Haiti
1,156,400

Santo Domingo,
Dominican Republic
2,240,500

Castries, St. Lucia
13,800

Port of Spain
Trinidad and Tobago
264,000

Bridgetown, Barbados
99,100

The number of people living in key Caribbean towns and cities.

Nassau, capital of the Bahamas. ▶▶ Most towns and cities in the region developed as tourist resorts.

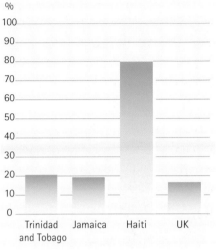

◄◄ A wooden shanty at Sandy Bay, in Jamaica. More than a third of Jamaicans live in poverty, mostly on the outskirts of large towns and cities.

 The percentage of people living in poverty in some Caribbean countries, compared to the United Kingdom.

Street Markets

People from urban and rural areas meet at the many fruit and vegetable markets. Country people bring surplus produce from their plots into the towns to be sold. The food on sale includes root vegetables, such as yams and eddoes, as well as plantains, bananas and squashes.

◄◄ Percentage of people working in agriculture.

In cities and countryside

Most of the poorest people in the Caribbean live on the outskirts of the cities, in small wooden houses that they have built themselves. Often these shacks or shanties do not even have a supply of electricity or any clean, piped water.

In the countryside people make a living by working on plantations, or they grow their own food on small plots of land.

Web Search ►►

► http://www.jis.gov.jm/
water_housing/
index.asp
Information about housing in Jamaica.

► http://www.jis.gov.jm/
land_environment/
index.asp
The geography of Jamaica.

► http://www.unesco.org/
focus/indcarib.html
Population figures from the United Nations Educational, Scientific and Cultural Organization.

Farming and Fishing

The Caribbean's warm, wet climate is excellent for growing sugar cane, coffee and bananas. Unfortunately, there is always the risk of violent storms that can destroy a valuable crop in minutes.

Good farming land is scarce in the Caribbean, so most of the islands need to import food. The smallest islands, such as the Caymans and the Turks & Caicos, rely on imports for almost all of their food.

Principal crops

The most important crops are sugar cane, bananas, coffee beans, cocoa and tobacco. Arrowroot is an important export for the island of St. Vincent. Crops are grown on estates or plantations, the largest covering 250 hectares or more, and exported all over the world.

In contrast to these large plantations, people who live in the countryside grow food on their own small plots of land, which are rarely larger than 3 hectares. On the smaller islands this is the only form of agriculture. The people keep a few hens, pigs, goats and in some cases a cow for milk. They grow traditional crops of sweet potatoes, plantains, yams and cassava.

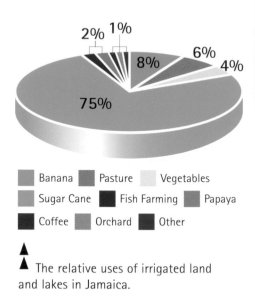

2% 1%
8%
6%
4%
75%

Banana   Pasture   Vegetables

Sugar Cane   Fish Farming   Papaya

Coffee   Orchard   Other

 The relative uses of irrigated land and lakes in Jamaica.

Sugar-Making

1. The sugar cane stalks are crushed for their sugary sap.
2. The cloudy sap is left in tanks to clear. Any solid particles sink to the bottom.
3. The clear sap is boiled to make a syrup.
4. The concentrated syrup is dried to produce brown sugar.
5. Refining and purifying this makes white sugar.

◄◄ A banana plantation on St. Lucia. The island produces over 70,000 tonnes of bananas each year.

12

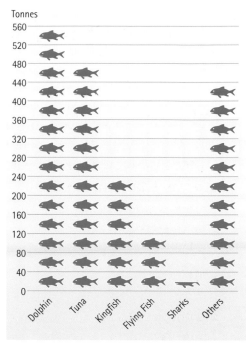

Tonnes

▲ Yearly fishing catches by boats from
▲ St. Lucia.

▲
▲ A fisherman off Grenada holds a
puffer fish that was trapped in his net.
This fish will be returned to the sea.

Food from the sea

The sea around the Caribbean islands is rich in fish, but
most are small reef fish that cannot be caught in large
enough numbers for commercial profit. Only a few fishing
grounds are suitable for large-scale fishing, so most of the
fish eaten in the region is imported.

Farming and Fishing

The only large-scale
fishing occurs around
the Bahamas.

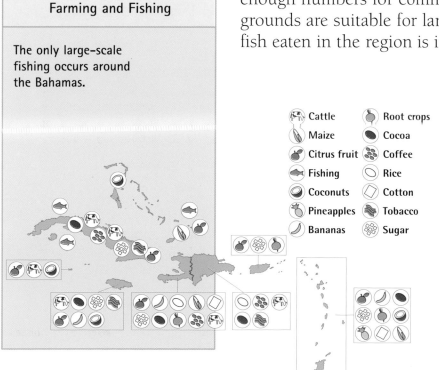

Cattle
Maize
Citrus fruit
Fishing
Coconuts
Pineapples
Bananas

Root crops
Cocoa
Coffee
Rice
Cotton
Tobacco
Sugar

Web Search ►►

► http://www.cbea.org
*Website of the Caribbean Banana
Exporters Association.*

► http://www.jamaican
coffee.gov.jm
About Jamaica's coffee industry.

► http://www.caricom-
fisheries.com
*Fishing industry profiles for all
CARICOM countries.*

Resources and Industry

The Caribbean attracts visitors from all over the world, but the region has other industries and resources besides the tourist business. International trade is very important, because the Caribbean has to import many of the goods that its people need.

Oil and gas contribute to the economies of Trinidad & Tobago and the Bahamas. These resources normally lie deep underground and have to be reached by drilling, but sometimes there is oil on the surface. Trinidad's 46-hectare Pitch Lake contains nearly 7 million tonnes of thick, black asphalt, which is exported for surfacing roads.

▲ Bauxite, a mineral containing aluminium, is mined in Jamaica. The island produces about $750 million of bauxite a year.

1.8% 1.4%

96.8%

Fossil Fuel Hydroelectricity Other

▲ The ways in which electricity is generated in Jamaica.

0.2%

99.8%

Fossil Fuel Other

▲ The ways in which electricity is generated in Trinidad and Tobago.

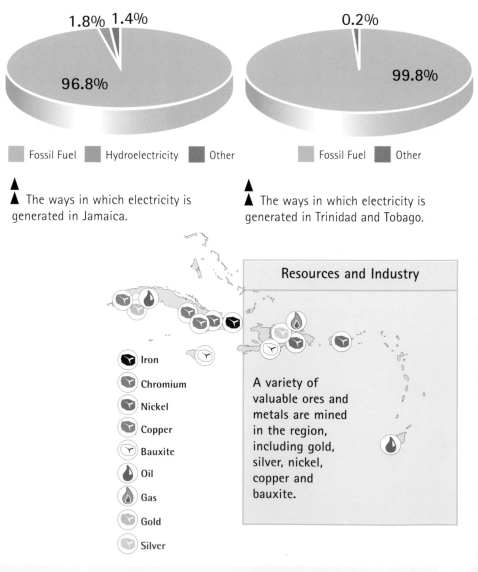

- Iron
- Chromium
- Nickel
- Copper
- Bauxite
- Oil
- Gas
- Gold
- Silver

Resources and Industry

A variety of valuable ores and metals are mined in the region, including gold, silver, nickel, copper and bauxite.

Tourism and other services

The Caribbean's most valuable natural resources are its tropical climate and beautiful landscapes. Sun, sea and sandy beaches attract millions of tourists to the region every year. More than 280,000 holiday-makers visit St. Lucia each year. Some of the islands earn most of their income from the tourist industry.

Another important service industry is banking. Foreigners are attracted to invest in Caribbean banks because of low taxes.

Sweet trade

The sugar-making business that was developed by the colonial powers in the 16th and 17th centuries is still one of the most important industries on Caribbean islands. Sugar and rum (an alcoholic drink made from cane sugar) are mainly exported to Europe. Other industries include clothing manufacture, furniture production and plastics.

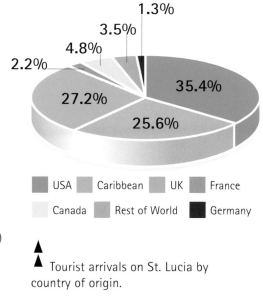

1.3%
3.5%
4.8%
2.2%
35.4%
27.2%
25.6%

USA | Caribbean | UK | France
Canada | Rest of World | Germany

Tourist arrivals on St. Lucia by country of origin.

Its warm, tropical climate makes the Caribbean a firm favourite with holiday-makers. Many tourists choose to island-hop on board huge, luxurious cruise ships. ▼

🌐 **Web Search** ►►

► http://www.gov.tt
Government site for Trinidad and Tobago.

► http://www.stats.gov.lc
Statistics from the St. Lucia government, including tourism figures.

► http://www.caribtourism.com
Information and links about Caribbean tourism.

Transport

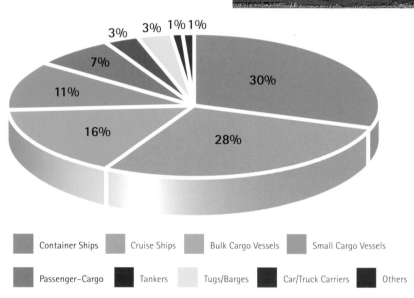

The Caribbean has a well-developed transport system. There are good air and sea links with the rest of the world and between the islands. Roads vary in quality, but are of a high standard in the towns.

Almost all of the islands have seaports to serve tourist cruise liners, inter-island ferries, yachts and leisure boats. Commercial harbours handle the international freight ships that bring in the goods and materials that are vital for the islands' survival.

Planes and trains

Many Caribbean islands have international airports with direct flights to and from the United States and Europe, while smaller airports offer flights between the islands.

A few of the islands have railway lines. These mostly serve the needs of sugar plantations and mines.

3% 3% 1% 1%
7%
11%
16%
30%
28%

Container Ships   Cruise Ships   Bulk Cargo Vessels   Small Cargo Vessels

Passenger-Cargo   Tankers   Tugs/Barges   Car/Truck Carriers   Others

▲ The principal types of ships visiting St. Lucia each year.

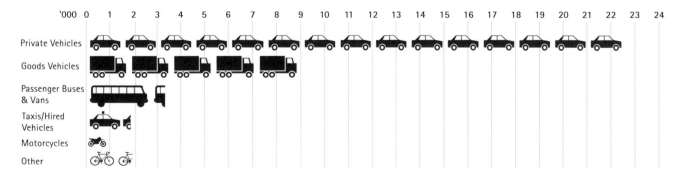

| | '000 0 | 1 | 2 | 3 | 4 | 5 | 6 | 7 | 8 | 9 | 10 | 11 | 12 | 13 | 14 | 15 | 16 | 17 | 18 | 19 | 20 | 21 | 22 | 23 | 24 |

Private Vehicles
Goods Vehicles
Passenger Buses & Vans
Taxis/Hired Vehicles
Motorcycles
Other

▲ Different types of road vehicles used on St. Lucia.

Passengers board an island-hopper at Canefield Airport, Dominica.

Road networks

The types of road on the islands vary widely. Those in the countryside may be little more than dirt tracks, while towns and cities have modern, paved highways.

The first roads were built to transport sugar and bananas to the ports. A network of smaller roads spread out from these freight routes. Buses and taxis operate on most of the islands today. Tourists also hire cars for getting around and sightseeing. In the countryside, donkeys and bicycles remain popular.

Road Traffic

On islands that were colonized by the French and Dutch (including the Netherlands Antilles, Guadeloupe and the Dominican Republic), vehicles are driven on the right. On islands that were colonized by Britain (including Jamaica, Barbados, Trinidad and Tobago and the British Virgin Islands) vehicles are driven on the left side of the road.

There are 18,700 kilometres of road in Jamaica and over 8,000 kilometres in Trinidad and Tobago. Barbados has just 1,600 kilometres of road.

Transport

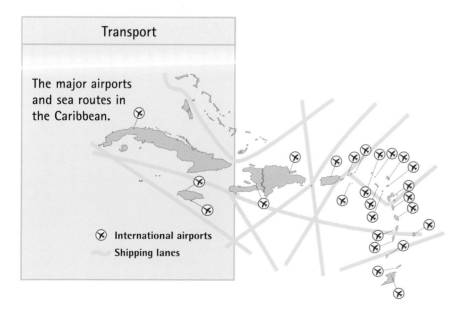

The major airports and sea routes in the Caribbean.

⊗ International airports
 Shipping lanes

Web Search ▶▶

▶ http://www.mtw.gov.jm
The Jamaican Ministry of Transport and Works.

▶ http://www.stats.gov.lc/index7.htm
Vehicle statistics for St. Lucia.

▶ http://www.tradetnt.com/tt/stats/transport.html
Flight and airport information for Trinidad and Tobago.

▶ http://www.airjamaica.com
Official website of Air Jamaica.

Education

Education levels vary across the Caribbean islands. Most schools can be attended for free and are run by the government. Children study a range of subjects including modern languages, maths, science and art.

Most schools in the former British colonies are run by government education departments. The larger islands also have a small number of private schools, where families pay for their children to be educated.

Children start school and change schools at the same ages as British and North American children and they sit similar examinations at the same ages. In Barbados, for example, children begin attending primary school at the age of four.

▲ Rates of literacy on various Caribbean islands.

◄◄ A secondary-school student in Barbados looks through a microscope during a science lesson. Science is a compulsory part of the curriculum.

Pupils at a primary school in St. Lucia. It is usual for Caribbean children to wear school uniform.

Secondary school

When children are 11 years old, they start secondary school. Barbados has 22 state secondary schools and most are co-educational – boys and girls study together. At the age of 16, students sit the Caribbean Examination Council (CXC) exams. Students who stay on at school after the age of 16 sit Advanced Level exams at the age of 18. Then, if their examination results are good enough, they can choose to carry on their studies at university, college or medical school.

Beyond school

The largest university in the region is the University of the West Indies. It has three main campuses (groups of university buildings) in Jamaica, Barbados and Trinidad, as well as smaller branches on other islands offering first-year tuition in a limited range of subjects.

On many islands, adults who have trouble reading and writing can attend adult literacy classes at night school.

 Web Search ►►

► http://www.cabinet.gov.jm/docs/MinEdCulture.htm
The Jamaican Ministry of Education and Culture.

► http://www.uwimona.edu.jm
The University of West Indies Mona campus.

► http://www.ncu.edu.jm
Northern Caribbean University.

Sport and Leisure

Caribbean athletes excel at the highest levels in international sport and track and field competition. The West Indies cricket team is world-famous, but other teams, including Jamaica's netball squad, are also becoming well known.

Tourists who visit the Caribbean enjoy the many sporting and leisure activities that are available throughout the region. The water sports include diving, snorkelling, windsurfing, powerboating, parasailing and swimming. Inland, people enjoy hiking, rock-climbing and horse-riding. Caribbean people enjoy these leisure activities, too. They also play other sports including football, netball, and their favourite, cricket.

Test Cricket

International cricket matches are known as test matches. They are played between the best cricket teams in the world. In the 10 years after 1976, the West Indies cricket team was almost unbeatable. It won all but two of the test matches it played.

Horse-racing at Bridgetown, Barbados. ▼

◄◄ Young boys practise cricket. Here, a boy sets up his position in front of the wicket before getting ready to play. The wicket-keeper stands in the background.

Winter sports

Caribbean athletes compete in many of the world's events, but the Caribbean climate makes it impossible to find the right conditions to practise for winter sports. Even so, a Jamaican bobsled team has competed in five Winter Olympic Games. In 2002, at the Winter Olympics held at Salt Lake City, USA, the Jamaican two-man bobsled team came 28th – a fantastic achievement.

Daily Life and Religion

Daily life in Caribbean cities is busy and noisy. In rural areas, fewer amenities (such as roads and running water) make life quieter but less comfortable. For many Caribbean people, religion is an important aspect of everyday life.

Daily life in the Caribbean varies from island to island and between the city and the countryside. Some countries are more developed and wealthy, while others are poorer and more rural. In most places the day begins with children going to school and adults going to work in the city or on the land. Families come together again after work and school to eat, rest and play.

◄◄ As elsewhere in the world, shopping is a popular pastime. These people are enjoying a colourful market at St. George's, the Grenadian capital.

22

Colonial religions

Most Caribbean people are Christian. Islands that were colonized by Roman Catholic Spain and France are still mostly Roman Catholic today. Islands colonized by Protestant Britain, such as Jamaica, Barbados and Trinidad & Tobago, are mainly Protestant. As a result of immigration from India, 23.8 per cent of Trinidadians are Hindu and 5.8 per cent are Muslim.

Voodoo and Rastafarianism

More than half of the population of Haiti practise voodoo, which mixes Roman Catholic and African beliefs.

Rastafarianism is another popular religion, practised especially in Jamaica. Rastafarians, or Rastas, believe that they belong to one of the lost tribes of Israel and worship the Hebrew God, whom they call Jah. They believe that one day they will return to their promised land in Ethiopia. There are about 100,000 Rastas in Jamaica.

At parish churches across Jamaica, such as this one at Mandeville, Protestants congregate each Sunday to worship. ▼▼

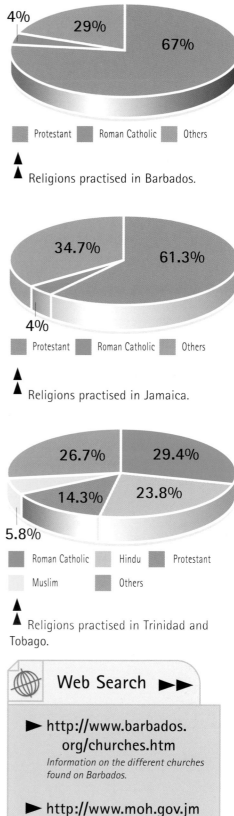

4% 29% 67%

Protestant ■ Roman Catholic ■ Others

▲▲ Religions practised in Barbados.

34.7% 61.3%

4%

Protestant ■ Roman Catholic ■ Others

▲▲ Religions practised in Jamaica.

26.7% 29.4%

14.3% 23.8%

5.8%

■ Roman Catholic Hindu ■ Protestant

 Muslim ■ Others

▲▲ Religions practised in Trinidad and Tobago.

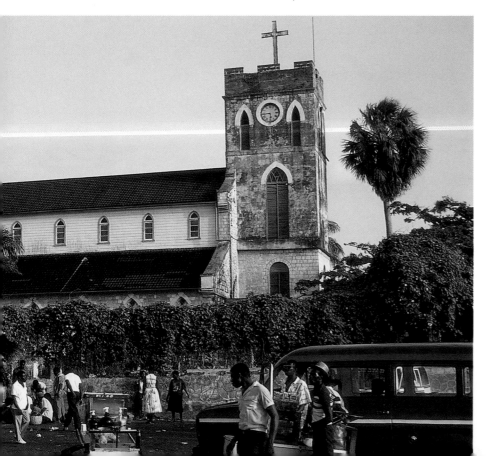

🌐 **Web Search** ►►

► http://www.barbados.org/churches.htm
Information on the different churches found on Barbados.

► http://www.moh.gov.jm
The Jamaican Ministry of Health.

Arts and Media

The numbers of radio and television stations on some of the main Caribbean islands.

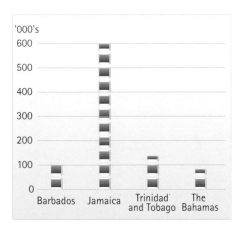

The number of people using the Internet on some of the main Caribbean islands.

►► At carnival time on Martinique, people dress up in colourful costumes and dance through the streets.

Home of reggae, calypso and the steel band, the Caribbean has a culture centred around music and dance. The region also boasts a strong literary tradition that has won acclaim throughout the world.

Caribbean music today can trace its roots back to rhythms, melodies and stories brought from Africa by slaves. One type of song, called calypso, originated in Trinidad. It started in the 19th century, with slave songs about unpopular people or unhappy experiences.

Trinidad was also the birthplace, in the 1930s, of a unique musical instrument – the steel drum. It is made from the end of an oil-drum that has been hammered into a shallow dish shape and divided into areas like a tortoise's shell. The size and shape of each area determines what sound it makes when hit by a rubber-tipped drumstick.

Carnivals held all over the Caribbean buzz with the energy, colour and heartbeat of Caribbean music, dance and costume. Carnival dates vary, but most take place around February and March and again in July and August.

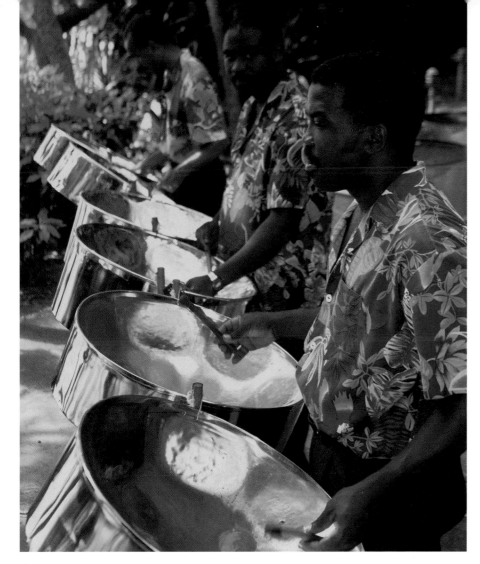

Musicians, dressed in typical colourful Caribbean shirts, play on steel drums.

Famous Caribbean Authors and Poets

Trinidad–born V S Naipaul (1932–) has set several novels in the Caribbean, including A House for Mr Biswas, The Mimic Men and Guerrillas.

St. Lucia's Derek Walcott (1930–) won the Nobel Prize for Literature in 1992. His poetry and plays explore his mixed–race background and the Caribbean's colonial history.

Samuel Selvon (1923–94) wrote about the lives and experiences of Indian immigrants to the Caribbean.

Andrew Salkey (1928–95), was raised in Jamaica and wrote plays, novels and poetry about Jamaican culture.

Web Search ▶▶

▶ http://www.everyting jamaican.com/ jamaica/music history.php
Information on the development of Jamaican music.

▶ http://www.jamaica observer.com
The Jamaica Observer newspaper.

▶ http://www.guardian. co.tt
The Trinidad Guardian newspaper.

▶ http://www.thenassau guardian.com
The Nassau Guardian newspaper, Bahamas.

Newspapers and broadcasting

Most Caribbean people enjoy freedom of speech and a free press. Many of the islands have their own newspapers, such as Jamaica's *Daily Gleaner* and *Jamaica Observer*. Other Caribbean newspapers include the *Trinidad Express*, the Bahamian *Nassau Guardian* and Barbados' *Daily Nation*.

Most islands have privately-owned radio and television stations, but Jamaica also has a state-run agency, the Jamaican Broadcasting Commission. Some commercial broadcasters, such as Radio Jamaica and the Caribbean Broadcasting Corporation, operate several different radio and television stations. Cable and satellite broadcasts from the United States can also be received in the Caribbean.

Government

The Caribbean is no longer ruled by the European nations that colonized it. Most Caribbean countries are now independently governed by their own elected representatives. However, they still keep close links with the former colonial powers.

As Caribbean countries developed their own identities and grew in confidence, they increasingly wanted to govern themselves instead of being ruled as colonies by European nations. In the 19th century the first countries to win their independence had to fight for it.

Then, during the 20th century, colonial government became less acceptable among the peoples of the world. One by one, the Caribbean colonies of countries such as Spain, the Netherlands and Great Britain were given their independence.

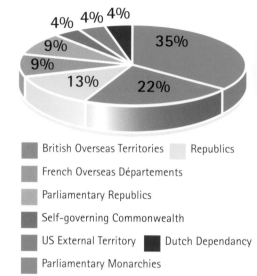

■ British Overseas Territories	□ Republics
■ French Overseas Départements	
■ Parliamentary Republics	
■ Self-governing Commonwealth	
■ US External Territory	■ Dutch Dependancy
■ Parliamentary Monarchies	

▲ The percentage of different types of government in the Caribbean region.

Invasion

The peace of the Caribbean was shattered in 1979 when a coup overthrew the government of Grenada, an independent country that was a British colony until 1974.
In 1983 a military force led by the United States invaded the island and democracy was restored.

▶▶ The government status of different countries in the Caribbean.

Government status

Country	Status	Since	Former status
Anguilla	British overseas territory	1982	British colony
Antigua and Barbuda	Parliamentary monarchy	1981	British colony
Bahamas	Parliamentary monarchy	1973	British colony
Barbados	Parliamentary monarchy	1966	British colony
British Virgin Islands	British overseas territory	1960	British colony
Cayman Islands	British overseas territory	1962	British colony
Cuba	Republic	1898	Spanish colony
Dominica	Parliamentary republic	1978	British colony
Dominican Republic	Republic	1865	Spanish colony
Grenada	Parliamentary monarchy	1974	British colony
Guadeloupe	French overseas département	1946	French colony
Guyana	Parliamentary republic	1966	British colony
Haiti	Republic	1804	French colony
Jamaica	Parliamentary monarchy	1962	British colony
Martinique	French overseas département	1946	French colony
Montserrat	British overseas territory	1960	British colony
Netherlands Antilles	Netherlands dependency	1954	Dutch colony
Puerto Rico	Self-governing commonwealth	1952	US possession
St. Kitts and Nevis	Parliamentary monarchy	1983	British colony
St. Lucia	Parliamentary monarchy	1979	British colony
St. Vincent and the Grenadines	Parliamentary monarchy	1979	British colony
Trinidad and Tobago	Parliamentary republic	1962	British colony
Turks and Caicos Islands	British overseas territory	1972	British colony
US Virgin Islands	US external territory	1917	Danish colony

Independence from Britain

Britain granted independence to many of its Caribbean colonies in the 1960s and 1970s. They chose a variety of different forms of government. Most of them became parliamentary monarchies. Each had its own parliament, but kept the British monarch as its head of state.

Three former British colonies, Trinidad & Tobago, Guyana and Dominica became parliamentary republics. They are each governed by a parliament with an elected president as head of state.

Five former colonies (Anguilla, the British Virgin Islands, the Cayman Islands, Montserrat, and the Turks & Caicos) became British Dependent Territories, which are today known as British Overseas Territories. This means that as well as an elected government they have a nominated British Governor who has some executive powers on behalf of the British Government.

▲ Labour force, in millions, of some of the main Caribbean countries.

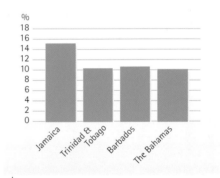

▲ Unemployment as a percentage of the total workforce.

◄◄ A soldier stands on guard outside the government offices in Nassau in the Bahamas.

Web Search ►►

► http://www.gov.tt
The official Trinidad and Tobago government website.

► http://www.stlucia.gov.lc
Website for the government of St. Lucia.

► http://www.caribinfo.com /government.html
The Caribbean home page for government information.

Place in the World

The Caribbean lies on a major shipping route that passes through the Panama Canal linking the Pacific and Atlantic Oceans. The different islands trade with each other and with countries all over the world. The region's natural beauty and tropical climate attract millions of visitors.

Caribbean countries belong to many of the most important international organizations, including the United Nations (UN), the World Health Organization (WHO), Interpol (the international police organization), Intelsat (an international satellite telecommunications organization) and the International Olympic Committee.

As former British Caribbean colonies became independent countries, they kept their close links with Britain. They joined a group of former British colonies from all over the world called the Commonwealth.

▼ The flags of some of the major
▼ Caribbean countries.

Dominican Republic   Jamaica   Bahamas

Trinidad and Tobago   Cuba   Barbados

The Palais de Justice (Law Courts) at Port de France on Martinique. French Départements such as Martinique and Guadeloupe are subject to French laws and elect representatives to the French parliament in Paris.

Caribbean power

Within the Caribbean, the most important organization is CARICOM (the Caribbean Community and Common Market). CARICOM makes decisions on economics and trade that apply to all of its member countries, with the aim of benefiting the whole region. CARICOM was formed in 1973 from an earlier organization, the Caribbean Free Trade Association (CARIFTA) that was set up in 1968 by eleven former British colonies.

When the Caribbean islands were seized by European powers in the 16th and 17th centuries, most of their trade was with Europe. Now, many Caribbean countries trade mostly with a bigger, closer market, the United States.

DATABASE

Chronology of Historical Events since the 1970s

1970s
Turks and Caicos islands become a British Dependent Territory; Bahamas, Grenada, Dominica, St. Lucia and St. Vincent and the Grenadines gain independence; coup in Grenada

1981
Antigua and Barbuda gains independence; the Organization of Eastern Caribbean States forms

1982
Anguilla becomes a British Dependent Territory

1983
St. Kitts and Nevis gains independence

1997–2000
Eruptions on Montserrat destroy Plymouth; volcanic activity continues

2004
Hurricane Ivan hits Jamaica and other Caribbean islands. More than 100 people are killed.

Web Search ▶▶

▶ http://www.oecs.org
The Organization of Eastern Caribbean States.

▶ http://www.jftc.com
Jamaica Fair Trading Commission.

▶ http://www.caricom.org
Website of the Caribbean Community and Common Market.

Gross Domestic Product (GDP) for various Caribbean islands.

The value of yearly exports from various Caribbean islands. ▼

These figures are for Jamaica, the Bahamas, Barbados and Trinidad and Tobago.

Total area:
30,488 sq km

Total population size:
4,401,520

Capital cities:
Kingston, Jamaica (588,700)
Nassau, Bahamas (180,000)
Bridgetown, Barbados (99,100)
Port-of-Spain, Trinidad and Tobago (264,000)

Other major cities:
Montego Bay, Jamaica
Freeport, Bahamas

Longest river:
Black River, Jamaica (71 km)

Highest mountain:
Blue Mountain Peak, Jamaica (2,256 m)

Jamaica's flag:
A gold saltire (diagonal cross) with two black and two green triangles. The gold represents the island's natural wealth and sunlight; the green, hope and farming resources; and the black, hardships overcome.

Official language:
English

Currencies:
Jamaican dollar (J$), Bahamian dollar (B$), Barbadian dollar (Bds$), Trinidad and Tobago dollar (TT$)

Major resources:
Bauxite, gypsum, limestone, natural gas, petroleum, asphalt, salt, timber

Major exports:
Bauxite, sugar, rum, alumina, bananas, coffee, cocoa, cement

Main public holidays:
New Year's Day (1 January)
Errol Barrow Day, Barbados (21 January)
Carnival, Trinidad and Tobago (mid-February to early March)
Spiritual Baptist Shouters' Liberation, Trinidad and Tobago (30 March)
Good Friday, Easter Monday (late March to late April)
Labour Day, Barbados (1 May)
Labour Day, Jamaica (23 May)
Indian Arrival Day, Trinidad and Tobago (30 May)
Labour Day, Bahamas (1st Friday in June)
Labour Day, Trinidad and Tobago (19 June)
Independence Day, Bahamas (10 July)
Kadooment Day, Barbados (1st Monday in August)
Independence Day, Jamaica (1st Monday in August)
Independence Day, Trinidad and Tobago (31 August)
Discovery Day/Columbus Day, Bahamas (12 October)
National Heroes' Day, Jamaica (16 October)
Independence Day, Barbados (30 November)
Christmas Day (25 December)

Religions:
Protestantism, Roman Catholicism, Hinduism, Islam

Glossary

AGRICULTURE
farming

ARCHIPELAGO
a group of islands

BIRTH RATE
the number of live babies born to every 1,000 people in a year

CLIMATE
the range of weather in a particular place over time

CURRICULUM
a programme of study

EXPORTS
goods sold to a foreign country

FOSSIL FUEL
a carbon-rich substance burned to release energy, such as coal, oil or gas

GOVERNMENT
the organization that makes the laws and rules that apply to a country

GROSS DOMESTIC PRODUCT (GDP)
the value of all the goods and services produced by a country in a year

HURRICANE
a powerful, destructive storm, also called a tropical cyclone, that often occurs in the Caribbean; hurricane-force winds blow at more than 160 kph

HYDROELECTRICITY
electricity generated by using flowing water to drive turbines, which turn electricity generators

IMPORTS
goods bought from a foreign country

INFANT MORTALITY RATE
the number of babies who die before the age of one, per 1,000 live births

LIFE EXPECTANCY
the average age when people die

LITERACY
a person's ability to read and write

MONARCHY
a form of government with a king or queen as head of state, though often ruled by an elected government

NEW WORLD
the western hemisphere, including North, Central and South America and the Caribbean

PARLIAMENT
a group of people elected to represent the population in a country's decision-making establishment

RELIGION
belief in, and worship of, a god or gods

REPUBLIC
a form of government, usually led by a president, in which the people or their elected representatives hold power

RESOURCES
the raw materials, land and people's skills that create a country's wealth

RURAL
describing the countryside

SUBSISTENCE FARMING
growing crops and keeping animals that are eaten mainly by the farmer's family, leaving little or no surplus to be sold

TROPICAL
the part of the Earth that lies between the Tropic of Cancer and the Tropic of Capricorn; 'tropical' can also mean hot and humid because of the weather conditions in the tropics

URBAN
describing towns and cities.

Index